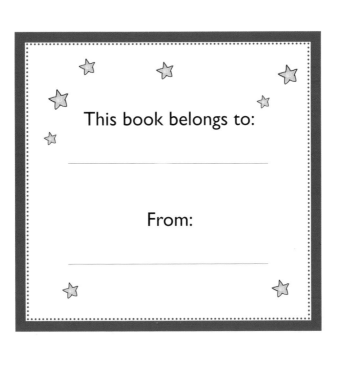

This book belongs to:

_____

From:

_____

Bedtime Blessings
for Girls

Carolyn Larsen
Illustrated by Caron Turk

christian
art kids

Contents

Dear Parents,

What's your family's bedtime routine?

Snuggling, reading and praying together with freshly bathed little ones are such special times when your children are small. Then there's the joy of peeking into their rooms and watching them sleep peacefully. What a delight!

Sending your children to bed with comforting thoughts of God's personal love and care for them certainly can help with that peaceful sleep. It is our hope that these gentle stories of God's generous blessings will help your children learn how much God cares for them and send them to bed with warm and comforting thoughts.

Enjoy these years of snuggling, reading and praying ... they go so fast, so, make a lot of memories!

Blessings,

Carolyn and Caron

God Made Everything!

God looked at everything He had made,
and it was very good.
Genesis 1:31

God made everything,
everything there is!
God made big, juicy caterpillars
and squishy, squashy jellyfish.
God made long and shiny snakes,
and ants that are tiny.
God made pebbles to skip
across a pond.
God made everything,
everything there is!

God made mountains with snow on the top.
God made deep, deep oceans filled with
fish, whales and octopuses.

God made the moon and stars to
shine at night-time.
God made the sun to
warm the daytime.
God made everything,
everything there is.
And best of all ...
God made you!

11

Sweet Thoughts
to Sleep On

God made the world because He loves you.
Enjoy the warm sunshine while you play in the park.
Enjoy the beautiful world God made!

★ What's your favorite animal God made?
★ Why do you like it so much?

Dear God,

Thank You for making the world.
Thank You for making everything
there is! Thank You for making me!

Amen.

God Is Your Helper

The LORD is with me to help me.
Psalm 118:7

Have you ever thought that you didn't need any help?
No help at all?
Have you discovered that you sometimes DO need help?

God will help you be kind to others.
He will help you when you are afraid in a storm.
God will celebrate with you when you are happy.
God wants to be your helper!

He will help you love others more and more too.
God knows obeying isn't always fun.
He will help you learn to obey Him.
He will help you obey your mom and dad too.

Sweet Thoughts
to Sleep On

Everyone needs help sometimes.
God wants to be your helper!
Just ask Him for whatever you need help with.

★ What has God helped you to learn?

Dear Father,

Thank You for helping me learn to obey You. Thank You for helping me learn to be kind to others.

Amen.

God Loves You

God is love. Those who live in love
live in God, and God lives in them.
I John 4:16

God loves you, did you know that?
Yes, He does and He shows you every day!
How can you know that God loves you?
Look around ... He made ponds that
you can skim rocks over.

He gave you a home to live in and
a family to take care of you.
God gives you daytime to play.
He gives you night-time to rest.

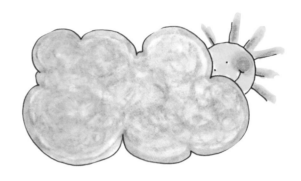

God made flowers and clouds and puppies
and kittens for you to enjoy!
God shows you every day
that He really loves you.

Sweet Thoughts
to Sleep On

God shows how much He loves you. He gives you things you need like food and water and special treats like rainbows and snowflakes. God likes to give you special things because He loves you so much.

★ What are some special ways God shows that He loves you?

Dear Father,

I know You love me because the Bible tells me that You do. But it's nice to think about all the things You give me and do for me every day.

Amen.

God Protects You

The LORD will keep you safe.
Proverbs 3:26

It's nice to know that someone is
taking care of you, isn't it?
Who takes care of you every day?
Your mom and dad take care of you.
They make sure you have food and a
home and a bed to sleep in.
They teach you rules to obey
that will keep you safe.

26

Did you know that God protects you too? He does!
He watches over you when you're playing outside.

He protects you when you're playing at a friend's house.
He watches over you when you're snuggled in bed.
God protects you because He loves you!

Sweet Thoughts
to Sleep On

You can rest easy tonight because God is taking care of
you. There is nothing for you to worry about.
Nothing will happen that God doesn't know about.

★ How does God take care of you each day?

Dear Father,

Thank You for taking care of me.
I'm glad to know You are always watching over me.

Amen.

Obeying God

You must obey the LORD your God
and do what He says is right.
Exodus 15:26

Obey. Obey. Obey. Does it seem like
you're always being told to obey?
Do you think that someday .... when you're
grown up ... you won't have to obey?
Did you know that even grown-ups have to obey? It's true!
There are laws and rules that everyone must obey.
The most important person to obey is God.
We learn how to obey God by reading the Bible.

God's most famous rules to obey
are the Ten Commandments.
Some of them teach us how to treat other people.
Some teach us how to treat God.

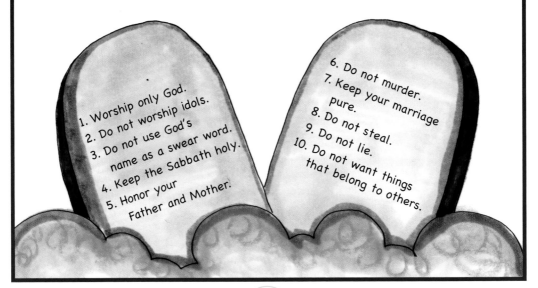

1. Worship only God.
2. Do not worship idols.
3. Do not use God's name as a swear word.
4. Keep the Sabbath holy.
5. Honor your Father and Mother.

6. Do not murder.
7. Keep your marriage pure.
8. Do not steal.
9. Do not lie.
10. Do not want things that belong to others.

Jesus said that the most important
rule is to love God.
The second most important rule is
to love other people.
Those sound like pretty easy rules to obey, right?

Sweet Thoughts
to Sleep On

Obeying God's rules helps everyone to be happier. Obeying God means you love other people. Obeying equals love!

★ Which Ten Commandment rule is the hardest for you to obey?

Dear Father,

Obeying isn't always easy.
But I want to show You that I love You.
So please help me to obey!

Amen.

Loving God

Love the LORD your God with all your heart,
all your soul, and all your strength.
Deuteronomy 6:5

When you love someone,
do you keep it a secret?
Of course not ...
you tell them so!
How do you tell God that
you love Him?

Do you dance a
twirling, swirling
happy dance?

Do you sing a loud,
joyful song of thanks?
Maybe you draw a big red
heart with lots of little hearts
around it.

It doesn't matter how
you tell Him — as long as
you tell Him.

Why do you love God so much?
Do you love Him for taking care
of you in the dark night?

Do you love Him for making the
sun to help flowers grow?
Do you love Him for giving you
a family and friends to enjoy?
No, you love Him for all these things,
and more! So ... tell Him!

Sweet Thoughts
to Sleep On

There are many reasons to love God.
He shows you every day how much He loves you.

★ What's your favorite way to show
God how much you love Him?

Dear Father,

Thank You for giving me so much.
I really love You and I want to
show You every day.

Amen.

Showing Love to Others

"Love each other."
John 13:34

Being kind. Saying nice things. Helping.
Obeying. Being patient.
These are all ways of showing love to others.
Some people are easy to love. But some are not.
Some people are grumpy. They say unkind things.
They are selfish. That's not nice!

Other people are easy to love. They are friendly
and kind. They always share. That's much nicer!
It's important to show love to everyone.
That's what Jesus did!

He said that anyone can love their friends. That's easy.
Only someone who loves God can love people
who aren't nice. That's harder.
Loving others shows we love God!

Sweet Thoughts
to Sleep On

God loves you — no matter what!
He said you should love other people too.
That means even people who may not be nice to you.

★ Can you name some people you love?

Bible

Dear Father,

Some people are hard for me to love.
I need Your help to love them.

Amen.

God Is Always With You

God has said, "I will never leave you;
I will never abandon you."
Hebrews 13:5

When you are snuggled in bed and fast asleep,
God is with you.
When your eyes pop open and a new day begins,
God is with you.
When you are playing at a friend's house,
God is with you.
When you are swinging in the park,
God is with you.

When the sun is shining and birds are singing,
God is with you.
When thunder is booming and lightning is flashing,
God is with you.
God is with you when you are all alone,
and when you are with your friends.
God is with you at church, and when you
are eating lunch with your family.

God is with you when you are yahoo-happy,
and when you are shh-quiet.
God is with you all the time, every minute
of every day and every night ...
Because He loves you very much!

Sweet Thoughts
to Sleep On

You are never ever alone.
God is with you all the time because
He loves you very much.

★ When does it help to remember
that God is with you?

Dear Father,

Sometimes it is scary to think about being alone. I'm glad to know that You are ALWAYS with me!

Amen.

God Sent Jesus

A child has been born to us;
God has given a son to us.
Isaiah 9:6

Did you know that God gave you a really special gift?
He did! God sent His Son, Jesus, to earth.
Jesus taught how to love and obey God.
Jesus showed how to love other people.

Some people didn't like Jesus. They were mean to Him.
They put Him on a wooden cross where He died.
But God brought Jesus back to life!

God sent Jesus to earth because He loves you.
God wants you to live in heaven with Him someday.
You can — because of what Jesus did.
Jesus was a really special gift, wasn't He?

Sweet Thoughts
to Sleep On

You can know that God loves you very much.
After all, He sent His very own Son to earth for you!

★ What would you like to say to God right now?

Dear Father,

Thank You for loving me so much.
Thank You for sending Jesus.

Amen.

God
Comforts You

God is the Father who is full of mercy and all comfort.
He comforts us every time we have trouble.
2 Corinthians 1:3-4

Have you ever had a very sad, not-so-good,
nothing-goes-right kind of day?
That's the kind of day when your best friend
gets mad at you – for no good reason!
On a nothing-goes-right kind of day you get in
trouble, but you don't know what you did!
Your puppy runs away, your favorite toy gets
broken, your prettiest shirt gets torn ...
it's a very sad, not-so-good,
nothing-goes-right kind of day!

What will make you feel better?
Who can help? Well, a hug from
Mommy or Daddy always helps.
But wait, Someone else loves you
very much too. He will help you!
Do you know who it is?
Do you want to take a guess?
Yes, it's God! He loves you more than
anyone else!

He will help your very sad, not-so-good,
nothing-goes-right kind of day turn right around!
How does He do that? He helps you
remember how much He loves you.
He helps you remember that His
strength is there when you need it.
He loves you, plain and simple.

Sweet Thoughts
to Sleep On

Sometimes the best way to get through
a hard day is to think good thoughts —
think about how MUCH God loves you.

★ What very sad, not-so-good, nothing-goes-right
kind of day have you had?

Dear Father,

Thank You for caring about my very sad,
not-so-good, nothing-goes-right kind of day.
Thank You for reminding me that You love me!

Amen.

God makes it better

Talking to God

"When you pray, you should pray like this:
'Our Father in heaven, may Your name always be kept holy.'"
Matthew 6:9

You learn what other people are thinking
when you talk with them.
Other people learn what you are
thinking by talking with you.

You talk with your mom and dad.
You talk with your friends.
But who else wants to talk with you?
God does!

Talking with God is called prayer.
He promised He would listen to you.
He promised that because He loves you.
The Bible tells us that is true!

God wants to know when you are happy.
He wants to know when you are sad.
He wants to know that you love Him.
Talk to God every day!

Sweet Thoughts
to Sleep On

God wants to know everything that's on your mind.
He loves you and wants to be your friend.
Talk to Him whenever you want.

★ What would you like to tell God?

Dear God,

I'm glad I can talk with You.
Thank You for hearing my prayers.
Thank You for loving me so much.

Amen.

Being Kind

Be kind and loving to each other,
and forgive each other.
Ephesians 4:32

Treat other people the way you
would like to be treated.
That's what Jesus taught.
Speak kind words to others.
You like to hear kind words, don't you?
Don't shout or say mean things
that will hurt someone's feelings.

Play nicely and share your toys.
That's more fun anyway, right?
You like it when your friends share with you, don't you?
Let your brother or sister go first in a game.
That is being kind.

Pick up your toys and put them away.
That helps your mommy and daddy.
Jesus said that being kind to others means
they will want to be kind to you.
That makes everyone feel happy!

Sweet Thoughts
to Sleep On

Being kind shows people that you like them.
Jesus treated others with kindness.
So when you are kind, you are being like Jesus!

★ When was someone kind to you?

Dear Father,

I want to be kind like Jesus is.
Help me to be kind,
even when I'm grumpy or tired.

Amen.

Being Patient

Always be patient.
Ephesians 4:2

Some friends don't play fair.
Some friends always want to go first.
Some friends want to play with your favorite toy.
Some friends always want to have their own way.

Are you patient with friends who behave this way?

Being patient means that you don't get angry
back – even when your friend gets mad.
It means you are kind when your friend
wants to play what she wants to play.
Being patient means thinking about
others instead of yourself.

Some people are patient with you when you
are selfish or do not play nice.
The most patient One of all is God!
God is really patient because He loves you.

Sweet Thoughts
to Sleep On

God is patient with you because
He loves you. Being patient with others shows
God's love to them.

★ When was a time that God was patient with you?

Mine!

Dear Father,

Sometimes I am selfish
and sometimes I am grumpy.
Thank You for
being patient with me.
Help me to be
patient with others.

Amen.

Praying for Others

Always pray for all God's people.

Ephesians 6:18

When your friend is sad, what can you do?
When your grandma is lonely, what can you do?
If your brother is scared, what can you do?
If someone you love is sick or has a problem
that is really big, what can you do?

You can't make a sick person well.
You can't always make a sad person happy.

Sometimes you just can't fix the problem.
But there is something you can do ...
something really special!
You can pray for your friend or loved one.
Praying means asking God to help. He wants to help!

God loves your friend or family
member even more than you do.
Praying for others is the absolute
best thing you can do!

Sweet Thoughts
to Sleep On

Pray for ...

Praying for others is the best way to help them ...
whatever their problems may be! God loves them too.

★ Who could you pray for right now?

Dear Father,

I'm glad I can pray for others. It's the best way to help them. Thank You for loving my family and friends even more than I do!

Amen.

Helping Others

Be ready to do good.
Titus 3:1

Helping is fun! Helping
makes me happy!
Helping makes me
smile. Helping others
is one of my favorite
things to do!
When I help others, it
makes them feel good.
It makes me feel good too.
What are some ways
I can help others?
I am a helper when
I pick up my toys.
I am a helper when I weed
the garden with Daddy.

I am a helper when I draw pretty pictures
for Grandma and Grandpa.
When I help others I am being like Jesus.

Jesus helped people when they were sad or sick.
Jesus helped everyone He could.
It must make Jesus happy when I am a helper too!

Sweet Thoughts
to Sleep On

Helping others is a nice thing to do.
Helping others shows that I love them!

★ What is one way that you can help someone tomorrow?

Dear Father,

Please help me to think of ways to be a helper.
Thank You for all the people who help me!

Amen.

1. Walk the dog
2. Clean my room
3. Feed the dog
4. Help Mommy
5. Put toys away

God Gives You
All You Need

God will use His wonderful riches in Christ Jesus
to give you everything you need.

Philippians 4:19

God knows what you need each day.
He gives you all that you need.
He gives you everything!
God gives you food and water
to help you grow.

He gives you ruffles and ribbons
and pretty hairbows.
God gives you Mommy and Daddy
to take care of you.
He gives you sisters and brothers,
grandmas and grandpas too!
Your friends are good gifts from God.
He gives you daytime so you can play with them.

Night-time for sleeping was God's idea too.
God gives you EVERYTHING you need!

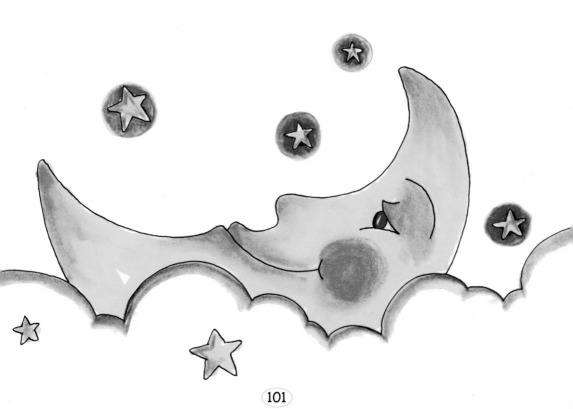

Sweet Thoughts
to Sleep On

God knows what you need each day.
Some of the things God gives are things you need to live.
Some things God gives just because He loves you.

★ What does God give you that you need each day?

Dear God,

Thank You for the special things You give me.
They show me that You think about me lots!
Thank You for loving me.

Amen.

God Forgives You

If we confess our sins, He will forgive our sins,
because we can trust God to do what is right.
I John 1:9

Everyone does wrong things sometimes.
Even grown-ups!
Sometimes things we do hurt other
people, like when we tell a lie.
These things hurt God, too,
because they break His rules.
Wrong things are called sin.

God is sad when we sin.
But He doesn't
get angry.

Do you know what God does? He forgives.
It's true! He will give you another chance to obey.
Do you know why He does that?
Because HE LOVES YOU!

God knows that the more chances you get
to obey, the more lessons you learn.
Then it is easier to obey the next time.

Sweet Thoughts
to Sleep On

God loves you very much. He is happy to forgive
you when you ask Him to. He will always
give you another chance to obey.

★ When has God forgiven you?

Dear Father,

Thank You for forgiving me and giving me more and more chances to obey.

Amen.

Being Unselfish

Do not look out only for yourselves.
Look out for the good of others also.
1 Corinthians 10:24

If you have a cookie but your friend
does not, what do you do?
Do you gobble it right up ... even the crumbs?
Or do you split it in half and share with your friend?
What if it breaks into one big piece and one little piece?
Do you give the little one or the big one to your friend?
Being unselfish means sharing your cookie.
It means offering the big piece to your friend.
Did you know that it feels good to be unselfish?

110

It feels good to be kind to others
and to share what you have.
Others will enjoy being with you
when you are unselfish.
They will learn to be unselfish too —
by your example.

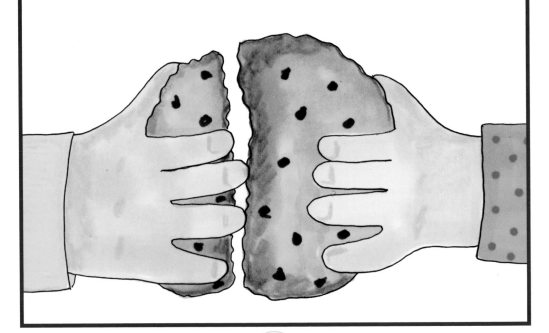

God is pleased when you are unselfish.
It shows that you care about others. He does, too.
Your love for God shines brightly when you are unselfish!

Sweet Thoughts
to Sleep On

Being unselfish means sharing with others.
It's the way God wants you to treat everyone!

★ When did someone unselfishly share with you?

Dear Father,

It isn't always easy to be unselfish.
Please help me to do better and better at it.

Amen.

Praising God

Let everything that breathes praise the LORD.
Psalm 150:6

Yippee, yahoo, hurray for God!
Praise God by telling Him how wonderful He is.
Praise God for bright rainbows after a storm.
Praise Him for playful puppies and kittens.

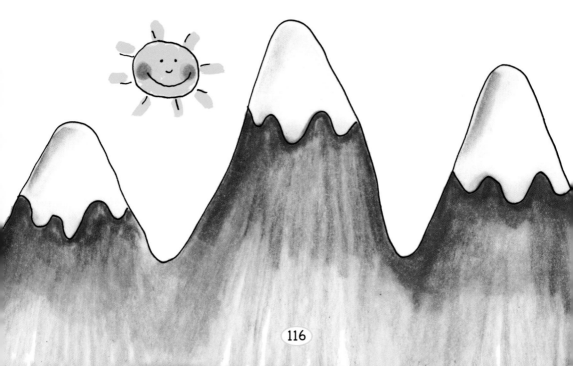

Praise God for red and purple
flowers swaying in the breeze.
Praise Him for moms and dads, and grandparents too.
Praise Him for friends to play with.

Praise God for the Bible that
teaches us about Him.
Praise Him for everything He
does to take care of you.
Praise Him most of all for ... Him!

Bible

Sweet Thoughts
to Sleep On

There are a million reasons to praise God. Everything you have and everything around you is a gift from Him!

★ What would you like to praise God for today?

Dear Father,

I'm glad to be reminded to praise You!
Thank You for all You give me and for loving me so much!

Amen.

Heaven Is a Wonderful Place!

"Rejoice and be glad, because you have a
great reward waiting for you in heaven."
Matthew 5:12

Heaven is an amazing place. It's where God lives!
Heaven is the most beautiful place you can dream of.
It's the happiest, most fun place ever!
Do you know something else about heaven?
God wants you to come live
there with Him someday.
For right now, though,
He has work for you
to do here for Him.
But someday,
you can live
in heaven — forever!

You can enter into God's heaven
because of what Jesus did.
He died for your sins, even though
He never did anything wrong Himself.

When you ask Jesus into your heart,
you can know that you will go to
God's wonderful heaven one day.

Sweet Thoughts
to Sleep On

If you have asked Jesus into your heart, then you can know for sure that you will go to heaven one day. Heaven will be amazing!

★ What do you think heaven will be like?

Dear Father,

Thank You that I can come to heaven someday. We'll have fun being together forever!

Amen.